P9-DIY-202

Fabulous FASHIONs of the 1960s

FELICIA LOWENSTEIN NIVEN

Fabulous FASHIONS of the DECADES

Enslow Publishers, Inc.
40 Industrial Road
Box 398
Berkeley Heights, NJ 07922
USA

http://www.enslow.com

Library of Congress Cataloging-in-Publication Data
Niven, Felicia Lowenstein.
    Fabulous fashions of the 1960s / Felicia Lowenstein Niven.
        p. cm. — (Fabulous fashions of the decades)
    Fabulous fashions of the nineteen sixties
    Includes bibliographical references and index.
    Summary: "Discusses the fashions of the 1960s, including women's and men's clothing and hair-
        styles, accessories, trends and fads, and world events that influenced the fashion"—Provided by
        publisher.
    ISBN 978-0-7660-3553-9
    1. Fashion—History—20th century—Juvenile literature. 2. Fashion design—History—20th cen-
    tury—Juvenile literature. 3. Lifestyle—History—20th century—Juvenile literature. 4. Nineteen
    sixties—Juvenile literature. I. Title. II. Title: Fabulous fashions of the nineteen sixties.
    TT504.N58 2011
    746.9'20904—dc22

                            2010004196

Paperback ISBN: 978-1-59845-279-2

Printed in the United States of America

052011 Lake Book Manufacturing, Inc., Melrose Park, IL

10 9 8 7 6 5 4 3 2 1

To Our Readers: We have done our best to make sure all Internet Addresses in this book were active
and appropriate when we went to press. However, the author and the publisher have no control over and
assume no liability for the material available on those Internet sites or on other Web sites they may link
to. Any comments or suggestions can be sent by e-mail to comments@enslow.com or to the address on
the back cover.

Every effort has been made to locate all copyright holders of material used in this book. If any errors or
omissions have occurred, corrections will be made in future editions of this book.

♻ Enslow Publishers, Inc., is committed to printing our books on recycled paper. The paper in every
book contains 10% to 30% post-consumer waste (PCW). The cover board on the outside of each book
contains 100% PCW. Our goal is to do our part to help young people and the environment too!

Illustration Credits: Advertising Archive/courtesy Everett Collection, pp. 22, 28, 32; AP Images,
pp. 4, 9, 11, 20, 41; AP Images/Mario Torrisi, p. 1; © Casey Hill/iStockphoto, p. 13; Dover Publica-
tions, Inc./Sears®, pp. 6, 7, 15, 16, 23; Everett Collection, pp. 27, 35; © INTERFOTO/Alamy, p. 33;
Library of Congress, pp. 43–45; Mirrorpix/courtesy Everett Collection, pp. 12, 40; Rue des Archives/
The Granger Collection, NYC — All rights reserved, pp. 19, 29; Shutterstock, pp. 5, 10, 21, 26, 31,
36, 47; Vernon Merritt III/Time & Life Pictures/Getty Images, p. 38.

Cover Illustration: AP Images/Mario Torrisi.

Contents

The 1960s

The 1960s

Three young women show off their paper dresses on the beach in 1966.

Wild and Crazy Fads

You probably can think of a lot of uses for paper. But would you make a dress out of it? A company did in the 1960s.

Scott Paper Company wanted to get their name out. They created a paper dress in two patterns. One was black and white; the other was red. Women could buy the dress for just one dollar and get coupons for Scott paper products.

People loved the idea. They could throw the dress out when it got dirty. They could hem it with a pair of scissors or fix it with tape.

Half a million orders poured in. It was too much for Scott Paper Company. After six months, they stopped making them. Other companies saw the chance, though. Mars Manufacturing Company became the leading maker of paper clothing. There were paper dresses for women and children, jumpsuits, evening gowns, and men's vests. People could even buy a paper wedding gown and waterproof paper raincoats and swimsuits!

Paper wasn't the only strange fabric used in the 1960s. You might say the materials were "space-age." There was a lot of talk about space travel. Americans had gone up in spaceships. People everywhere watched the progress to the moon. Designers took note, making clothes from shiny vinyl and using the color silver. They also experimented, linking together metal or plastic discs to make dresses and designing full-length bodysuits. People walked around looking like space-age heroes.

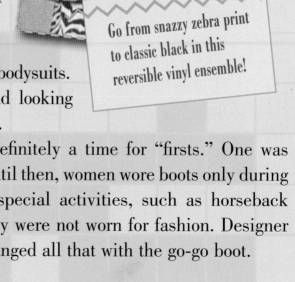

Go from snazzy zebra print to classic black in this reversible vinyl ensemble!

The 1960s was definitely a time for "firsts." One was women's boots. Up until then, women wore boots only during bad weather or for special activities, such as horseback riding or hiking. They were not worn for fashion. Designer Andre Courreges changed all that with the go-go boot.

Go-go boots go with everything, from classy skirts to playful jumpers.

FABULOUS FASHIONS of the 1960s

Go-go boots were made from shiny vinyl or plastic. They had a low heel and a zipper up the back. Popular in white, they went up as far as the calf, knee, or even higher. Go-go boots were perfect for the short hemlines of the time.

Granny glasses were another popular accessory. These round glasses first appeared in the 1960s. They were worn by famous people, such as musician John Lennon. They caught on with young people. Many tinted their glasses in colors like pink and orange.

These were just some of the wild and crazy fads of the 1960s. After all, the 1960s was to be one of the most open-minded decades in history. It was also a great time to be young. People were enjoying a good economy. There was a feeling of freedom. Because times were good and money was plentiful, people paid more attention to fashion than ever before.

Chapter 1

Hairstyles

In the 1960s, hair was short—and long. Women wore it in trendy above-the-shoulder cuts. They also sported it shoulder length. Longer hair was put in a neat ponytail. Sometimes it was decorated with flowers or ribbons.

Women could also tease, or back comb, their hair to give it some height. High hair was very stylish indeed. In the 1960s, many women teased their hair. They set it in large rollers. They also used a lot of hair spray to keep it in place.

Women and men also straightened their hair. They used relaxing creams. Don't be confused by the harmless sounding name: the creams included harsh chemicals.

A popular man's hairstyle, called the conk, depended on a chemical called lye. It was worn by African Americans who wanted their hair to look sleeker. The lye would burn scalps as well as straighten hair.

This unique style combined the height and the sleekness of the 1960s by having half the hair piled high on top of the head and the other half hanging down the shoulder.

For everyday use, there was a blow-dryer. This was an early version of today's handheld blow-dryer. Some models included hoses that connected to a plastic cap. Due to technology, from better electric motors to the use of plastic, these home blow-dryers were lighter and more powerful than ever before. They were also more colorful.

Hairstyles

The sixties was clearly a decade concerned with hair. If you lived back then, you might have worn one of these hairstyles. Which one would you choose?

Girls Flipped for the Pageboy

You may know the pageboy haircut. It is when the hair is cut just below the ears and then curled under. Women could choose to have bangs or not.

But it wasn't just the pageboy that was popular in the sixties; it was the pageboy flip. That meant that the hair was not curled under but rather curled out the opposite way to create the flip. First Lady Jackie Kennedy wore the pageboy flip. Millions of women copied her style.

First Lady Jackie Kennedy sported the elegant pageboy flip. She was a fashion icon in the 1960s.

The Modern Look: Five-point Bob

Vidal Sassoon created a new type of bob in 1963. In the original bob, the hair was cut straight across. Sassoon cut different angles instead. He actually cut them into the hair,

Vidal Sassoon cuts fashion designer Mary Quant's hair into a five-point bob.

so they would fall into place easily. Not only was it a unique shape, but the hair also stayed that way without bobby pins or hair spray.

The Buzz About the Bouffant and the Beehive

Have you ever teased your hair? That is when you comb it back, moving the comb down the hair toward the scalp. Teasing causes the hair to stick up, and that was how women

It took some work and a lot of hair spray to create a bouffant!

13

created the bouffant and beehive hairstyles. The hair was teased so it was high on the head. Women also used "rats," rolls of real or fake hair, to make their hair bigger. Hair spray was used to keep it in place.

Bouffants were high hairstyles. Beehives were similar but went even higher. They looked like a beehive, which is how the style was named. Sometimes women set their hair in large curlers, about the size of soda cans, to help add height.

Top Teen 'Dos

Do you like your hair long and loose? You would have fit right in during the sixties. Most teens wore it that way. They might have worn a headband to keep their hair tidy. One ponytail on the side was also very popular. Hair might be wrapped over the elastic, or it might be tied with a ribbon. There were no hair "scrunchies" yet.

Straight hair was also in style. But it was hard to get if it did not come naturally. There were no hair-straightening irons. Girls who wanted straight hair sometimes used creams that straightened hair. You already heard about African-American men and the conk style. African-American women, too, used powerful chemicals to change the texture of their hair.

Chapter 2

Women's Styles and Fashion

Most people remember sixties' fashions as pretty colorful. However, they did not start out that way. The early years were rather boring, with clothes that seemed to be made for older adults. Then, small shops started a new trend. They sold cheap, flashy clothes that attracted young people, who started buying. For the first time in history, the young were leading trends in fashion.

In the 1960s, women were able to wear different styles. Their fashion told you about them. Some women were beatniks, or outsiders. Beatniks wore a lot of black. They wore black turtlenecks, tight black pants, and berets. Beatniks generally kept to themselves.

PANTS 'N TOPS CAPTURE
THAT LONG, LEAN LANKY LOOK

Tweed, plaid, and turtlenecks were conservative alternatives to the funky colors and designs that emerged.

That was not the case with hippies. Hippies were rebellious young people who did not agree with corporate America. They did not like war or other government decisions. Their protests were loud and frequent.

You would know a hippie not only by what he or she said but also by the way that he or she dressed. Hippies wore long skirts or flowing robes, tie-dye shirts, and dresses. Their clothing had fringes and beads. Hippies also decorated everything, even their bodies. Women and men dressed alike. In a way, that made it easy to treat women and men more like equals.

You didn't have to be a hippie or a beatnik to have a specific kind of look. Some women dressed to celebrate their heritage. For example, African-American women would wear African clothing, bright cottons in bold prints.

Many women simply dressed in the modern way with vivid colors, geometric shapes, and short hemlines. The new decade was here, and women were ready.

A Flare for Fashion: Bell-bottoms

One popular style was the bell-bottom pant that became wide, or flared out, at the knee and continued getting wider as the leg went down. These pants were not really new; they had been around before, worn by sailors because their wide legs made them easy to roll up. They were named bell-bottoms because the shape was a little like a bell.

Bell-bottoms became a style embraced by the hippies. They liked to wear them with brightly colored shirts. The style became a symbol of the hippie generation and peace and love.

The Skinny on the Jean

Women's jeans were popular during this time, and they would never be mistaken for men's jeans. While men had the zipper in the front, women's zippers were sometimes in the back or on the side. Also, women's jeans were formfitting. Unlike bell-bottoms, the skinny jeans fit tight against the leg all the way down.

Less Is More

Tight was definitely "in" during the sixties. So was short. It was the perfect time for the miniskirt. Designer Mary Quant was not the first to make a miniskirt, but she helped make them popular. She liked the shorter hemline. Her skirts were six to nine inches above the knee. Quant designed ones with lace patterns and open mesh. Other designers soon followed suit. There were miniskirts everywhere, in every conceivable color or pattern.

The young people loved them. They wore the skirts with high boots or patterned tights. They may have even liked that their parents and grandparents disapproved of them!

British designer Mary Quant is most famous for popularizing the miniskirt, a style still found in the closets of many women today.

Split It With Culottes
(rompers)

There were pants, and there were skirts. Then, there was the fashion that was a little bit of both. Culottes are split skirts. In the 1960s, they were a loose-fitting design that went down to a woman's calf.

It was like wearing flowing pants. Culottes had the freedom of pants but they looked more formal, like a skirt. However, culottes were considered too casual for school. Sometimes, though, they could pass if they looked enough like a dress or skirt.

Culottes came in many different lengths and styles, such as this polka-dotted one-piece from designer Anne Fogarty's spring 1967 collection.

20

Chapter 3

Men's Styles and Fashion

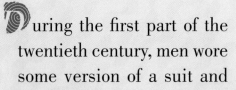

During the first part of the twentieth century, men wore some version of a suit and tie. But colors were dull, and there were not a lot of choices. That all changed in the 1960s. Finally, men had a chance to flex their fashion muscle!

The first changes were small. Suit lapels and pants both became narrower. No longer did men have to wear hats everywhere they went. Hats were more formal. They were not needed during this time of fresh, new casual attitudes.

The young people loved the changes. But young men wanted to express themselves even further. So they wore their suits with a new type of shoe that had a pointy toe and a funny name: "winkle picker."

It wasn't long before suits were made in brighter colors, and in stripes and patterns. Men paired them with colorful shirts and ties. And if they did not want to wear a tie, they could wear a sports jacket with a turtleneck.

Near the end of the sixties, styles for men became really fancy. Men wore wider, more colorful ties than ever before. They also wore ascots, or neck scarves. They chose shirts in bold patterns and fluorescent colors. These patterns and colors were not just on their shirts. They were on their pants, too. It was a fun time for men's fashion. They had as many choices as women.

Men could mix different colors and patterns on button-down shirts and ties to create their own unique looks.

Not Just for Turtles

Turtleneck sweaters were once popular in the Victorian period and again in the 1920s. They were in style again in the sixties. Men wore them with sports jackets in place of a shirt and tie. The turtlenecks weren't as formal as the shirt and tie, but they still looked neat and presentable. Men could make them look even more casual if they paired them with jeans.

Just as they do today, turtlenecks came in all different colors. Beatniks preferred them in black. But if a man wasn't a beatnik, any color was game. Men in the sixties would probably have several different colors in their closets.

Turtlenecks, especially black ones, look sophisticated yet casual when paired with plaid hipster trousers.

23

What Is a Winkle Picker?

You might wonder what *winkle picker* means. *Winkle* is a British term. It describes something pointed. The shoes' pointed ends were the reason for the name.

Not only was the name different, but the shoes were, too. In fact, they looked a little like ladies' shoes! They also looked like the footwear worn in medieval times.

But winkle picker shoes were definitely a fit for the 1960s. They were a good match for the new narrow hipster pants. They were also a way for young men to have fun with fashion.

The Sixties' Sports Jacket

Do you know the difference between a suit jacket and a sports jacket? A suit jacket exactly matches pants that go with it. It is considered a more formal look. A sports jacket is not worn with matching pants. It creates a more casual and cool look.

In the sixties, sports jackets were more popular than suits because they allowed men to mix and match colors and fabrics and express their personal style. The jackets were often made from different materials and colors. Sports jackets could be seen in suede, corduroy, and velvet, for example, and in a variety of shades. Men would pair them with pants of contrasting colors and even fabrics.

The sports jackets of the sixties were both single-breasted and double-breasted. Single-breasted meant that the two sides met in a single row of buttons. Double-breasted meant the front came together so that part of it overlapped. There was a double row of buttons to fasten it. Both were popular looks for the time.

Going Wide

How wide is a tie? If you said a couple of inches, you would be right—and wrong. Ties come in different widths; usually, it depends on the fashion at the time. In the late sixties, ties became very wide—up to five inches across. They also had bold patterns. For example, ties might be polka-dotted, have colorful stripes, or even have bright flowers!

Chapter 4

Accessories

The 1960s were all about color. One might expect to see a bright orange purse worn with an orange dress and even orange shoes. But there were also a lot of patterns. There were stockings in different colors, and the dress could be in a different color, too. So when a woman wore it all together, she did not look like an orange!

The sixties' woman matched those bright colors with colorful makeup. Blue and green eye shadows were popular. So were false eyelashes. They came in black, brown, and other colors.

Hippies moved away from designers. Handmade articles became so popular that they spawned an arts and crafts movement. People did macramé, knotting cord and beads into jewelry and purses. They tie-dyed T-shirts and scarves.

Accessories

New handbag styles came out. They were made from many different materials other than dull leather. Handbags could be found in straw or wicker, velvet, or patent leather. Flowers and shells were popular decorations, and so were fake jewels.

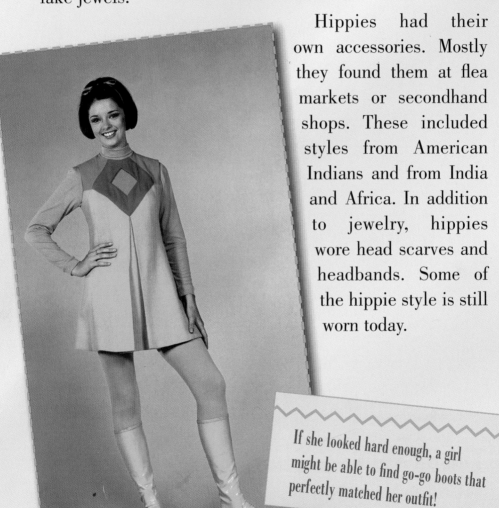

Hippies had their own accessories. Mostly they found them at flea markets or secondhand shops. These included styles from American Indians and from India and Africa. In addition to jewelry, hippies wore head scarves and headbands. Some of the hippie style is still worn today.

If she looked hard enough, a girl might be able to find go-go boots that perfectly matched her outfit!

Real or Fake?

Many women wore false eyelashes in the sixties. They made eyes look dramatic. That was the style of the makeup back then. The focus was on the eyes. There were brightly colored eye shadows, and lips were done in softer colors.

False eyelashes were made of plastic and came with glue. Women glued them onto their eyelids. Only sometimes the glue did not work too well. Many women who visited the bathroom found an eyelash stuck to her cheek instead!

Real hair lashes for 9/11!

Another beautiful bargain from Miners. Real hair lashes for just 9/11*. And in either Black or Brown. 'Lower Lashes': the great new thing for eyes. And three super styles for upper lids – 'Flashy Lashes', 'Natty Lashes' and 'Roundy Lashes'. Lashes you can't afford not to get!
*Recommended retail price.

miners
young make-up shake-up

Some cosmetics companies make false eyelashes from real human hair!

The Headband

Headbands were not just for women in the sixties. Men wore them, too. The sixties' headbands were worn close to the forehead, and sometimes across it in hippie-style.

They were made of many different materials. This could include strings of flowers, fringed leather, or cloth. Some were thin and beaded. They were easy to make by hand but so popular that they could be bought almost anywhere.

Shiny Steps

Today you might find patent leather shoes in black or white. The sixties went a little farther. They had red, white, blue, hot pink, orange, green, and yellow. Want a yellow patent shoe with red highlights? You could probably find it back then. The shoes had rounded toes and chunky heels. Some had ties or buckles, and many had matching purses.

American actress Sharon Tate (1943–1969) looks hippie-chic in a brightly colored cloth headband!

Love Those Legs

Colorful stockings were just what those bold shoes needed. They were also seen with the short hemlines. Stockings came in all colors, patterns, and textures. Some even had words, such as "love," on them. The stockings came in knee-high or full-length styles. They were very comfortable.

Then there were panty hose. No longer did women have to wear girdles and suspender belts to hold up their nylon stockings. They could pull on a pair of panty hose. They stretched all the way up to the waist. The panty hose did not even have a seam in the back, as the old stockings did. This was new for the 1960s, and it became all the rage.

Chapter 5

Fads and Trends

The freedom in the sixties meant people could dress however they liked. One could be conservative like First Lady Jacqueline Kennedy in a neutral-colored two-piece suit and pillbox hat. Or maybe one would choose a beatnik's dark clothes. Some might like the beaded, fringed look of a hippie. Others could even try some styles from other countries. By 1967, the stores were filled with Asian styles, such as harem and tent dresses and Nehru jackets. Then there was pop art fashion, which used popular photos or other images on clothes. There also was bright, colorful psychedelic fashion. Some fashion choices were inspired by science-fiction films and books. There were new, futuristic-looking materials, such as a type of plastic called PVC, that were turned into wearable fabric. Polyester and vinyl were also used.

Designers experimented with all sorts of new fashion—including a see-through dress! There was clearly something for everyone. Which would you choose?

The New Nehru

Indian clothing was popular during this time. The Nehru jacket was named after Jawaharlal Nehru, prime minister of India, who often was seen wearing this style of clothing. The Nehru jacket featured a stand-up collar and no lapels. It was smooth from neck to waist. Both men and women wore Nehru jackets.

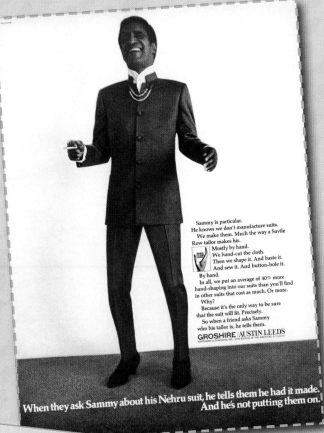

Sammy is particular.
He knows we don't manufacture suits.
We make them. Much the way a Savile Row tailor makes his.
Mostly by hand.
We hand-cut the cloth.
Then we shape it. And baste it. And sew it. And button-hole it.
By hand.
In all, we put an average of 40% more hand-shaping into our suits than you'll find in other suits that cost as much. Or more.
Why?
Because it's the only way to be sure that the suit will fit. Precisely.
So when a friend asks Sammy who his tailor is, he tells them.
GROSHIRE/AUSTIN LEEDS

When they ask Sammy about his Nehru suit, he tells them he had it made. And he's not putting them on.

American entertainer Sammy Davis Jr. (1925–1990) rocks a Nehru suit!

Fashion Meets Art

Modern abstract art came alive in the sixties. There were paintings made of geometric shapes and bold colors, and designers took note. Yves Saint Laurent looked at a painting by an artist named Mondrian. It was bold with a black grid against white. Some of the blocks were colored red, blue, and yellow. He decided to make a dress that looked just like it. Women knew the painting and saw it on the dress. It had never been done before and caused some excitement.

No need to visit a museum to view works of art! Yves Saint Laurent's "Robe Mondrian" brought abstract art into women's closets in the mid-sixties.

Other designers took their cue from Yves Saint Laurent and used art in their clothes. Some used images from popular culture, and others created bold black-and-white patterns. These designs appeared on everything from T-shirts to dresses and hats.

Now You See It

A lot of designers tried new ideas. One in particular, Betsey Johnson, decided to do something really different. What if she made a dress that was completely see-through? It was a radical concept, but she did it. She created it out of clear vinyl. And because a woman would look naked wearing a clear dress, she included paste-on stars or numbers or fish. Women could put them anywhere they wanted, to cover the parts they did not want people to see.

It was a crazy idea but it worked. People made a big fuss over it. They were ready for more crazy ideas. That is about the time of the world's first topless swimsuit, designed by Rudi Gernreich. He also made a swimsuit that came with thigh-high boots. Most ordinary people did not wear these fashions, but they loved to talk about them!

Going Psychedelic

The word *psychedelic* comes from the Greek word *psyche*. It refers to the mind. In fashion, it has come to mean bright colors and patterns. There was plenty of that in the sixties.

Sometimes the colors were so bright that they glowed. Neon blues, greens, and purples were used by designer Emilio Pucci, who liked to design in those colors. Cartoons and fantasy drawings became part of this style.

American actress and singer Leslie Uggams lights up the TV screen in this psychedelic dress!

Chapter 6

Pop Culture

The sixties are famous for being a time of peace and love. You could tell by looking at the hippie fashions and listening to the songs and poetry of the time. But it was also a time of war. That was also reflected in popular culture. The United States was fighting in Vietnam in Southeast Asia. Not everyone agreed about going to war; there were many public protests against it. The popular slogan "flower power" reflected people's wishes to end the bloodshed.

On the home front, there was other violence. The decade was a time of assassinations, or killings. Among them were President John F. Kennedy, his brother presidential candidate Robert Kennedy, and activists Martin Luther King Jr. and Malcolm X. The killings were tragic. They brought the nation together to mourn.

Science was also at the forefront during this time. It made it possible for men to go to the moon. Space travel was an exciting part of the sixties. It influenced fashion, too.

The music of the decade revealed some new sounds and some powerful messages. People welcomed groups, such as the Beatles. Many also witnessed the largest rock concert in the history of the world at Woodstock.

The fashions of the time reflected what was going on. Fashion often offers great clues about social change. A lot can be told about what is going on by the way people dress.

The Black Identity

In the 1960s, African Americans began to celebrate their cultural identity. In the past, they might have copied what could be considered traditonally Caucasian styles, from straightening hair to wearing the same types of clothes. Now they were ready to be different.

This came at a time when African Americans were fighting to be treated the same as whites. There were still places in America that separated the races. They simply wanted the same opportunities and treatment.

Their clothes became a statement of pride. They reflected their culture. For example, African Americans might combine traditional African cloth with modern styles. Kente fabric was used in everything from T-shirts to robes and bow ties.

A young man dressed in an African-inspired leopard print suit and hat chats with a more conventionally dressed young lady on the streets of New York City in 1969.

African-American pride helped create the black arts movement. This was a movement that celebrated African-American writers, poets, playwrights, and artists.

The Fab Four and Fashion

Chances are that you have heard of the Beatles. Most people consider them a groundbreaking band that ushered in a new style of music. They also helped create some new fashions.

Nicknamed the "Fab Four," the Beatles were made up of four young men from Liverpool, England: John Lennon, Paul McCartney, George Harrison, and Ringo Starr. They had a modern sound and clever lyrics. They charmed people on both sides of the Atlantic. They became so popular that they caused hyper reactions from their fans. Young women screamed and fainted at their concerts.

The Beatles' mop-top haircut was widely copied. It looked like a mop, with hair hanging down over the forehead and past the ears. The cut was so popular that toy makers produced Beatles' wigs.

The Beatles' collarless suits and ankle boots with pointed toes were also popular. The look was known as "mod," a modern fashion trend for young people. Later, during the psychedelic period, the look would change. Again, fans would copy the bright colors and floral and paisley prints of their idols' clothing. They also copied the Indian-style collarless shirts and sandals worn by the group.

Three big Beatles fans wear dresses featuring their idols' faces as they wait for their favorite group to come out of a movie premiere in 1964.

Woodstock

On August 15, 1969, about half a million people came together at the Woodstock Free Festival of Art and Music, more than a hundred miles from Manhattan on a farm.

Woodstock was a three-day rock concert. The organizers were young and hadn't done anything like this before. But they had the money to attract some of the best-known bands around. Jefferson Airplane, The Who, Creedence Clearwater Revival, Sly and the Family Stone, Santana, Jimi Hendrix, and Janis Joplin all performed.

Music fans sit on top of a painted microbus at Woodstock, a concert famous for its message of peace, love, and rock and roll.

It turned out to be the world's largest concert of its kind. But that wasn't all. It became a symbol of the hippie generation. Even today, the fashion is associated with a free-spirited time.

A film of the concert shown in Europe helped create a hippie movement overseas. Fashions at Woodstock included collarless shirts, cheesecloth and Indian cotton dresses, headbands, and beads.

Man on the Moon

Ever since humans looked up in the sky, we have dreamed about space travel. It became a reality in the sixties, when the space race got going. The United States and Russia both wanted to put a man on the moon. Who would do it first?

On July 20, 1969, we had the answer. The Americans landed *Apollo 11* on the surface of the moon. Our astronauts took those first steps. They planted an American flag for all to see.

"That's one small step for man, one giant leap for mankind," astronaut Neil Armstrong said proudly.

Astronauts Edwin "Buzz" Aldrin and Neil Armstrong wore space suits made of twenty-one high-tech layers of material. Most were synthetic, or man-made. This led the way for other modern textiles.

Timeline

The 1920s

The look: cloche hats, dropped-waist dresses, long strands of pearls (women), and baggy pants (men)

The hair: short bobs

The fad: raccoon coats

The 1930s

The look: dropped hemlines, natural waists, practical shoes (women), and blazers and trousers (men)

The hair: finger waves and permanents

The fad: sunbathing

The 1940s

The look: shirtwaist dresses and military style (women) and suits and fedoras (men)

The hair: victory rolls and updos

The fad: kangaroo cloaks

The 1950s

The look: circular skirts and saddle shoes (women) and the greaser look (men)

The hair: bouffants and pompadours

The fad: coonskin caps

The 1960s

The look: bell-bottoms and miniskirts (women) and turtlenecks and hipster pants (men)

The hair: beehives and pageboys

The fad: go-go boots

The 1970s

The look: designer jeans (women) and leisure suits (men)

The hair: shags and Afros

The fad: hot pants

The 1980s

The look: preppy (women and men) and *Miami Vice* (men)

The hair: side ponytails and mullets

The fad: ripped off-the-shoulder sweatshirts

The 1990s

The look: low-rise, straight-leg jeans (both women and men)

The hair: the "Rachel" cut from *Friends*

The fad: ripped, acid-washed jeans

The 2000s

The look: leggings and long tunic tops (women) and the sophisticated urban look (men)

The hair: feminine, face-framing cuts (with straight hair dominating over curly)

The fad: organic and bamboo clothing

Glossary

abstract—A style of art that is the opposite of realism; it uses shapes and colors but no realistic images.

accessories—Items that are not part of your main clothing but worn with it, such as jewelry, gloves, hats, and belts.

beatnik—A rebellious, artsy person who usually dresses in black.

beehive—A hairstyle similar to the bouffant, but worn even higher on the head.

bell-bottoms—Pants that flared out at the knee and continued getting wider as they went down.

bob—A woman's short haircut.

bodysuit—A tight-fitting one-piece garment.

bouffant—A hairstyle in which the hair is teased and worn high on the head.

conk—A hairstyle in which the hair is chemically straightened.

ethnic—Relating to a group that shares a common culture.

fad—A craze that happens for a brief period of time.

flare—To become wider at the bottom edge.

geometric—Describes such shapes as rectangles, squares, and circles.

hippie—A rebellious person who rejects conventional society, is antiwar, and usually has long hair.

leisure—Relaxation.

miniskirt—A short skirt that ends above the knee.

pageboy—A hairstyle in which the hair is cut just below the ears and then curled under or, in the case of the pageboy flip, flipped out.

trend—The general direction in which things are heading.

vinyl—A type of plastic.

vivid—Intensely bright.

Further Reading

Books

Connikie, Yvonne. *Fashions of a Decade: The 1960s.* New York: Chelsea House, 2007.

Jones, Jen. *Fashion History: Looking Great Through the Ages.* Mankato, Minn.: Capstone Press, 2007.

Niedler, Alison A., and Jim Heimann. *Fashion of the 20th Century: 100 Years of Fashion Ads.* Los Angeles, Calif.: Taschen America LLC, 2009.

Rooney, Anne. *The 1950s and 1960s.* New York: Chelsea House, 2009.

Internet Addresses

Fashion-Era, "1960s Fashion History"
<http://www.fashion-era.com/the_1960s_mini.htm>

Paperpast Yearbook, 1960
<http://www.paperpast.com/html/1960_fashion.html>

Index